America, My Country
Explorers

Christopher Newport

By Moira Rose Donohue

Clarke C. Scott, M.A.
Content Consultant

STATE STANDARDS PUBLISHING LLC

Your State • Your Standards • Your Grade Level

Dear Educators, Librarians and Parents . . .

Thank you for choosing this *"America, My Country"* book! We have designed this series to support state Departments of Educations' Common Core Standards for curriculum studies AND leveled informational text. Each book in the series has been written at grade level as measured by the ATOS Readability Formula for Books (Accelerated Reader), the Lexile Framework for Reading, and the Fountas & Pinnell Benchmark Assessment System for Guided Reading. Images, captions, and other design and critical thinking elements provide supportive visual messaging and learning activities to enhance text comprehension. Glossary and Word Index sections introduce key new words and help young readers develop skills in locating and combining information. We wish you all success in using this *"America, My Country"* series to meet your student or child's learning needs.

Jill Ward, President

Publisher

State Standards Publishing, LLC
1788 Quail Hollow
Hamilton, GA 31811
USA
1.866.740.3056
www.statestandardspublishing.com

Cataloging-in-Publication Data

Donohue, Moira Rose.
　Christopher Newport / Moira Rose Donohue.
　　p. cm. -- (America, my country explorers)
　Includes index.
　ISBN 978-1-93881-305-4 (lib. bdg.)
　ISBN 978-1-93881-309-2 (pbk.)
　1. Newport, Christopher, ca. 1565–1617--Juvenile literature.　2. Virginia--Discovery and exploration--Juvenile literature.
　3. Explorers--Virginia--Biography-- Juvenile literature.　4. Explorers--Great Britain--Biography-- Juvenile literature.
　5. Virginia--History--Colonial period, ca. 1600–1775--Juvenile literature.　6. Jamestown (Va.)--History--Juvenile literature.
　7. Ship captains--Great Britain--Biography--Juvenile literature.　I. Title.
　975.5/01092--dc23　[B]

2013934114

About the Author

Moira Rose Donohue has a Bachelor of Arts degree in political science from Mississippi University for Women and a Juris Doctorate degree from Santa Clara University School of Law. She was a banking legislative lawyer for 20 years before she began writing for children. Moira is a published author of numerous poems, plays, and articles, as well as two picture books. She loves dogs and tap dancing, and lives in northern Virginia with her family.

About the Content Consultant

Clarke C. Scott holds degrees from Central Michigan University and has 33 years of experience as a classroom teacher, building principal and system-wide administrator. Clarke most recently served as Director of Middle School Education and Lead Director for History with Pittsylvania County Schools in Virginia. He enjoys hiking, kayaking, caving, and exploring Virginia's and our nation's history. He shares his adventures both above and underground with his wife, Joyce, and family.

About the Cover Image – Did Newport Have a Hook?

Our cover image is a reproduction of a well-respected artist's interpretation depicting historical aspects of the landing at Jamestown – and showing Newport with a hooked right hand. While the loss of a portion of Newport's arm is well-documented, his use of a hook has now been called into question by many historians.

1 2 3 4 5 – CG – 17 16 15 14 13

Table of Contents

Hi, I'm Bagster! Let's learn about Explorers.

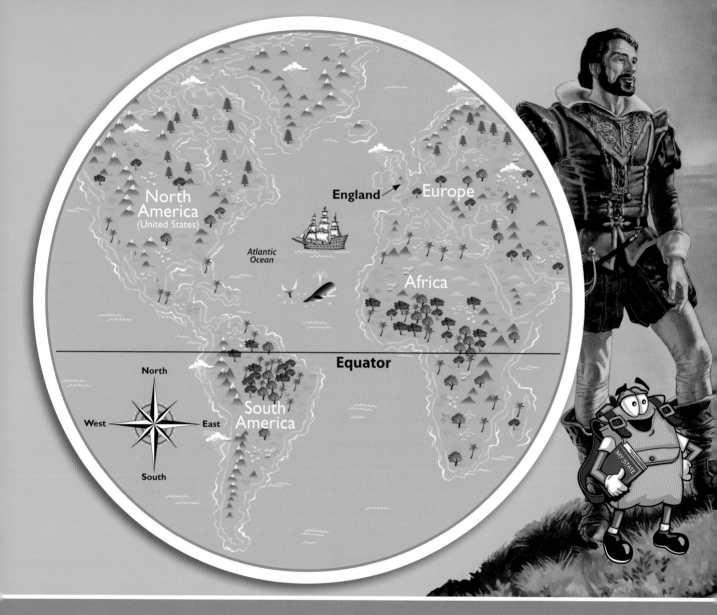

North America
(United States)

Atlantic
Ocean

England → Europe

Africa

Equator

North

West   East

South

South
America

Christopher Newport was born in Europe in the country of England.

Time Line

**1560
or 1561**
Born

When He Was a Lad

Christopher Newport was born in Europe in the country of England. No one is sure whether he was born in 1560 or 1561. Records back then were not complete. Christopher lived in the town of Harwich. It is on the coast of the North Sea.

Christopher's father and uncle were sailors. They taught Christopher how to sail, too. Christopher learned to understand the wind. He learned about the tides and currents in the ocean. Christopher also learned to use a **compass** and an **astrolabe**. A compass tells the direction the ship is sailing. A sailor's astrolabe tells how far away a ship is from the **equator**. The equator is an imaginary line around the center of the earth. These were important tools for **explorers**, who look for new discoveries.

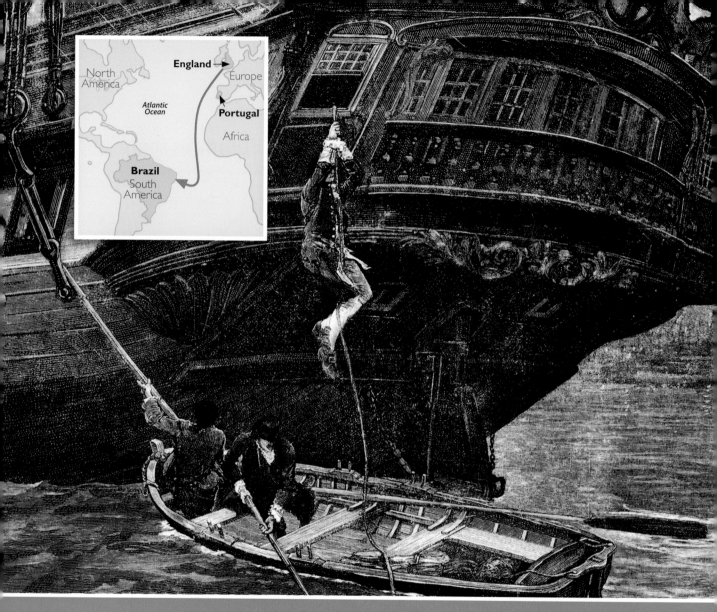

Christopher and his friends jumped ship in Brazil.

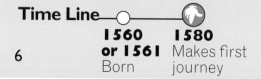

Time Line

1560
or 1561
Born

1580
Makes first
journey

Jumping Ship

Records show that Christopher first went to sea in 1580. He sailed on an English ship named the *Minion*. The captain of the ship was a firm man. The crew didn't like him. The *Minion* sailed to Brazil in South America. When it sailed close to land, Christopher and two friends "jumped ship." They went ashore without permission. They never returned to the ship.

Settlers from the country of Portugal were living in Brazil. They were not friendly to the English and chased the *Minion* away. Christopher didn't want to get caught by the settlers. And he wanted to get home. Christopher was very brave and very clever. And somehow, he got home! Back in England, he became a sea captain's **apprentice**. He worked for the captain. He learned to **navigate**, or set a ship's course. He also learned about commanding a ship during storms and other hard times.

Queen Elizabeth gave privateers permission to attack Spanish ships.

Time Line

1560 or 1561	1580	1590
Born	Makes first journey	Becomes captain

Pirates of the Caribbean?

In 1568, Spaniards attacked an English sea captain in Mexico. The queen of England, Elizabeth I, wanted to get back at Spain. She allowed the captains of private English ships to attack Spanish ships and settlements. The captains had to give the queen a part of any treasure they found. These captains and their crews were called **privateers**.

In 1584, Christopher married Katherine Proctor. They lived in a part of London called Limehouse. Katherine died several years later. After her death, Christopher sailed as a master's mate, or helper, on a privateering ship called the *Drake*. In 1590, he was given command of a privateering ship called the *Little John*. He became the ship's captain.

It's a Fact!

Sometimes the privateers attacked non-Spanish ships. That made them pirates, matey. Arrrgh!

The Spanish ship sank!

It's a Fact! Europeans called the Americas the New World.

Christopher and his men attacked a Spanish ship filled with silver.

Time Line

1560 or 1561	1580	1590
Born	Makes first journey	Becomes captain

Captain Hook?

Christopher made several journeys to the West Indies. These islands in the Caribbean Sea are part of the Americas. Europeans called the Americas the **New World**. On his first trip, Christopher sailed with three other ships. Soon, the ships separated as they found Spanish ships to attack. Christopher and his men attacked one Spanish ship filled with silver. But the Spaniards didn't give up easily. They fought back. The English finally won the fight. But the Spanish ship sank! The English crew couldn't get much of the treasure.

During the fight, part of Christopher's right arm was cut off. Even though he lost part of his arm, Christopher chased several other Spanish ships. Unfortunately, he didn't find much treasure.

It's a Fact!

Some people think Christopher was the model for the character named Captain Hook in James Barrie's play, *Peter Pan*. But many historians today think Christopher did not use a hook.

Christopher helped capture the *Madre de Dios* and its treasure!

Time Line

1560 or 1561	1580	1590	1592
Born	Makes first journey	Becomes captain	Captures treasure ship

The Time Has Come

Christopher never joined the other English ships. They had gone to check on the English settlement at Roanoke Island in present-day North Carolina. But Christopher stayed in the Caribbean to look for more treasure. Then he returned to England.

In 1592, Christopher was hired to command the *Golden Dragon*. He sailed to the West Indies again. On the way back to England, Christopher spotted a ship called the *Madre de Dios*. It was full of treasures from the New World. Christopher said to his men: "Masters, now the time is come that either we must end our days or take the said carrack (ship)." With several other English ships, Christopher helped capture the *Madre de Dios* and its treasure! The *Madre de Dios* was Christopher's biggest prize. He was now a wealthy man. And he was about to get richer.

It's a Fact!

When the other English ships arrived at Roanoke Island, everyone had disappeared! The only clue was the word "CROATOAN" carved on a tree. What happened there is still a mystery today.

King James I made peace with Spain.

How did Christopher's life change when King James made peace?

Christopher started trading in the New World.

Time Line

1560 or 1561	1580	1590	1592
Born	Makes first journey	Becomes captain	Captures treasure ship

14

Crocodiles and Kings

Christopher had married a second time. But his second wife died, too. Christopher then married a rich woman named Elizabeth. They had four children. In 1596, he bought part of his own ship, the *Neptune*, for privateering.

James I became king of England after Queen Elizabeth I died. King James made peace with Spain. Now there was no more privateering. Christopher started trading in the New World. He knew the king liked unusual animals. Christopher brought the king two baby crocodiles. King James wanted to settle the New World and find riches. He set up the Virginia Company to start a colony there. He also wanted to find a path across the Atlantic Ocean to Asia. This was called the **Northwest Passage**. The Virginia Company chose Christopher to lead the trip. He knew more about sailing to the New World than almost anyone in England.

It's a Fact!

Crocodile or alligator? Only the crocodile has two long lower teeth you can see when its mouth is closed. But don't get close enough to look!

The colonists landed on Powhatan Indian territory.

Christopher commanded three ships that sailed to the new colony at Jamestown.

Time Line

1560 or 1561	1580	1590	1592	1607
Born	Makes first journey	Becomes captain	Captures treasure ship	Arrives at Jamestown

Jamestown

Christopher commanded all three ships on the journey—the *Susan Constant*, the *Godspeed*, and the *Discovery*. He was given a sealed box. A secret list inside named the colony's leaders. Christopher was told not to open the box until he landed. In 1607, 104 colonists arrived in present-day Virginia. They sailed into the Chesapeake Bay to the mouth of today's James River. They started a settlement there called Jamestown.

When he arrived, Christopher opened the sealed box. His name was on the list of seven leaders. Christopher's job was to explore Virginia's rivers. He sailed up the James River as far as the waterfalls near today's Richmond. The waterfalls along the rivers marked America's **Fall Line**. This steep strip of land makes a natural boundary. The Fall Line prevented further travel on the river. Christopher was one of the first explorers to sail this far.

It's a Fact!

America's Fall Line runs from Alabama to New Jersey. Can you guess why many towns were started here?

17

Christopher sailed into a storm and was shipwrecked on Bermuda.

Time Line

1560 or 1561 Born	1580 Makes first journey	1590 Becomes captain	1592 Captures treasure ship	1607 Arrives at Jamestown	1609 Crashes on Bermuda

Shipwrecked!

Christopher sailed back to England to get supplies. When he returned to Jamestown in 1608, he found that more than half of the colonists had died from hunger or sickness. Christopher helped the colony and made friends with Powhatan. He was the leading chief of many Indian tribes in the area.

Christopher went back again for supplies and settlers. In 1609, he made a fourth trip to Jamestown. He was captain of one of the ships named the *Sea Venture*. It sailed into a storm. Christopher helped steer the ship to the island of Bermuda. Everyone survived, but the ship sank. Sadly, the colonists at Jamestown had almost no food during the winter. This was called the "Starving Time." The settlers on Bermuda built two boats from cedar trees and parts of the old ship. In the spring, Christopher sailed to Jamestown with the healthy settlers.

It's a Fact!

One of Christopher's passengers, John Smith, caused trouble on the trip. But his name was on the secret list. John became a leader in the Jamestown colony.

Christopher's shipwreck set the path for a settlement on Bermuda.

Christopher helped start Jamestown, the first permanent English settlement in North America.

Time Line

1560 or 1561 Born	1580 Makes first journey	1590 Becomes captain	1592 Captures treasure ship	1607 Arrives at Jamestown	1609 Crashes on Bermuda	1617 Dies

The Worthy Seaman

Christopher went back to England for supplies once more. He made a total of five trips to Virginia. Then he went to work for a trading company called the East India Company. Christopher made three journeys to Asia. He traded for silk cloth and spices. In 1617, Christopher got sick and died in Asia.

Christopher was an excellent sailor. A friend called him "a worthy seaman and commander." Christopher didn't discover riches in the New World or find the Northwest Passage. But he helped start the colony at Jamestown, Virginia, and was one of its leaders. Jamestown became the first permanent English settlement in North America. And remember how Christopher saved people when his ship crashed on Bermuda? This set the path for a settlement there later. Today, a university in Virginia is named after Christopher Newport.

Glossary

apprentice – A student who is learning a job from a skilled worker.

astrolabe – A sailor's tool that tells how far a ship is from the equator.

compass – A tool that finds direction using a magnetic needle.

equator – An imaginary line around the center of the earth.

explorer – A person who travels seeking new discoveries.

fall line – A natural boundary of sloping land. America's Fall Line runs from Alabama to New Jersey. It separates the flat Coastal Plain from the Piedmont region on higher ground. Rivers create waterfalls over a fall line.

navigate – To set the course, or direction, of a ship.

New World – The name Europeans called the Americas. The New World includes the continents of North America and South America.

Northwest Passage – A pathway across the Atlantic Ocean that allows sailors to travel northwest from Europe to Asia.

privateer – A sailor on a private ship who has permission to attack an enemy ship.

Sound It Out!

Caribbean: **care-ih-bee-uhn**
Croatoan: **crow-ah-tow-an**
Madre de Dios: **mah-dray day dee-ohs**

Powhatan: **pow-ha-tan**
privateers: **pry-vuh-teerz**

Say these words like a pro!

Word Index

Editorial Credits

Designer: Michael Sellner, Corporate Graphics, North Mankato, Minnesota
Consultant/Marketing Design: Alison Hagler, Basset and Becker Advertising, Columbus, Georgia

Image Credits — *All images © copyright contributor below unless otherwise specified. Maps: Edward Grajeda/iStockphoto unless otherwise specified.*

Cover – Newport*. **4/5** – Newport*; Map: John Woodcock/iStockphoto; Ship: David Crooks/iStockphoto. **6/7** – Sailors: North Wind Picture Archives. **8/9** – Queen: Queen Elizabeth I/FineArtAmerica; Pirate: Claus Danner/Alamy. **10/11** – Galleons & Roanoke: North Wind Picture Archives; Peter Pan: "Fight with the Pirates" from "Peter Pan," Strobridge, American School/Collection of the New York Historical Society, USA/BridgemanArtLibrary. **12/13** – Ship: "The Spanish Armada," by Peter Jackson/Private Collection/Look & Learn/BridgemanArtLibrary. **14/15** – Trading: North Wind Picture Archives; James: John de Critz/Wikipedia; Crocodile: WorldsWildlifeWonders/Shutterstock. **16/17** – Newport Landing*; Powhatans: Picture Collection, New York Public Library, Astor, Lenox & Tilden Foundations; Fall Line: PhotoTreat/iStockphoto. **18/19** – Ship: Mary Evans Picture Library; Smith: Traveller1116/iStockphoto. **20/21** – Jamestown: North Wind Picture Archives; Bermuda: Richard Goerg/iStockphoto. **24** – Globe: Globe: Alfonso de Tomas/Shutterstock.

* A mural depicting Captain Christopher Newport at Newport News Point on May 2, 1607, was commissioned in 1955 for the 350th anniversary of the Jamestown Landing. Hampton, Virginia, artist Allan D. Jones Jr. created a 27-foot-long oil painting that is hanging inside the West Avenue Library, 2907 West Avenue, Newport News, Virginia. The library is listed on the State and National Registers of Historic Places because of its beautiful Georgian Revival architecture and because of its significance in the social history of Newport News. It has been operating as a library since officially opening on Oct. 14, 1929. The mural was restored in 2007 by Mark Lewis with the Chrysler Museum of Art for the 400th anniversary of the Jamestown Landing. Newport News (Va.) Public Library System photo.

Explore With Bagster

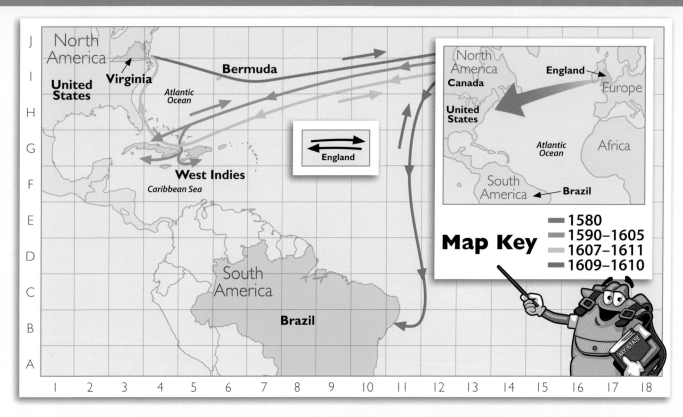

Map labels:
- North America
- United States
- Virginia
- Bermuda
- Atlantic Ocean
- West Indies
- Caribbean Sea
- South America
- Brazil
- England

Inset map labels:
- North America
- Canada
- United States
- England
- Europe
- Atlantic Ocean
- Africa
- South America
- Brazil

Map Key
- 1580
- 1590–1605
- 1607–1611
- 1609–1610

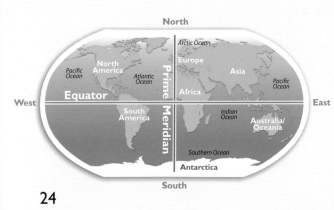

Globe diagram labels:
- North
- Arctic Ocean
- Europe
- Asia
- Pacific Ocean
- North America
- Atlantic Ocean
- Africa
- Prime Meridian
- Equator
- West
- East
- South America
- Indian Ocean
- Australia/Oceania
- Southern Ocean
- Antarctica
- South

Words You Should Know!

continent – One of the great divisions of land on the earth. The seven continents are: Africa, Antarctica, Asia, Australia/Oceania, Europe, North America, and South America.

equator – An imaginary line around the center of the earth that divides the Northern Hemisphere from the Southern Hemisphere.

hemisphere – Half of a sphere (the globe) created by the equator or the prime meridian. The four hemispheres are: Northern, Southern, Western, and Eastern.

ocean – A vast body of salt water. The five oceans are: Arctic, Atlantic, Indian, Pacific, and Southern.

prime meridian – An imaginary line around the center of the earth that divides the Western Hemisphere from the Eastern Hemisphere.